THE
DOUBLE EDGED SWORD

Copyright © 2023 by Jeff Williams

Published by Four Rivers Media

All rights reserved. No portion of this book may be reproduced, stored in a retrieval system, or transmitted in any form or by any means—electronic, mechanical, photocopy, recording, scanning, or other—except for brief quotations in critical reviews or articles, without prior written permission of the author.

All Scripture quotations are taken from the NIV Holy Bible, New International Version®, NIV®. Copyright © 1973, 1978, 1984, 2011 by Biblica, Inc.™ Used by permission of Zondervan. All rights reserved worldwide. www.zondervan.com. The "NIV" and "New International Version" are trademarks registered in the United States Patent and Trademark Office by Biblica, Inc.™

For foreign and subsidiary rights, contact the author.

Cover design by Sara Young
Cover photo by Andrew van Tilborgh

ISBN: 978-1-960678-95-9   1 2 3 4 5 6 7 8 9 10

Printed in the United States of America

JEFF WILLIAMS

THE DOUBLE EDGED SWORD

CUTTING TO THE HEART OF YOUR BUSINESS AND YOUR LIFE

A 40-DAY DEVOTIONAL

CONTENTS

Introduction 9

PART I. ACHIEVING SUCCESS IN BUSINESS 13

DAY 1. The Birthplace of Great Ideas 15

DAY 2. Momentum Has a Friend Named Discipline 19

DAY 3. Walking on the Edge 23

DAY 4. Worshipping Success Jeopardizes Success 25

PART II. ENGAGING PEOPLE IN BUSINESS 31

DAY 5. Your Heart Is Meant to Be Shared 33

DAY 6. Beware of the Water Ski Effect 37

DAY 7. Lending Your Belief 41

DAY 8. Find Out What They Know 43

PART III. FAITH IN BUSINESS 47

DAY 9. God Will Find You Every Time 49

DAY 10. Relationship with God Is Not the End Goal 53

DAY 11. Delight Begets Blessing 57

DAY 12. Dare to Die the Second Death 61

DAY 13. Letting Go Doesn't Mean Giving Up 65

PART IV. GENEROSITY IN BUSINESS 71

DAY 14. Giving Starts the Flow 73

DAY 15. Questions to Guide Your Giving 77

DAY 16. The Secret Behind the Secret 81

PART V. GROWTH IN BUSINESS 87

DAY 17. People before Production 89

DAY 18. Two Degrees at a Time 93

DAY 19. Put Each Problem in a Box 97

DAY 20. We Are Asking the Wrong Question 101

DAY 21. Build Through It to Get Through It 105

PART VI. HANDLING PEOPLE 111

DAY 22. Every Day you Ice a Team 113

DAY 23. Put a Number on Their Head 117

DAY 24. Not a Savior, but a Walker 121

DAY 25. The Question that Turns Criticism into a Close 123

DAY 26. Which Battle Will You Lose? 127

DAY 27. Surprise Them with a Thank You 131

PART VII. HIGHER THINKING 137

DAY 28. Will You Survive, Strive, or Thrive? 139

DAY 29. What You've Reaped, You've Sown 143

DAY 30. One Idea Deserves Hours of Thought 147

DAY 31. Provide Solutions, Not Just Services 151

PART VIII. INSPIRATION 157

DAY 32. Hope Has a Family 159

DAY 33. There's No Place Like the Present 161

DAY 34. Significance Starts with You 165

PART IX. LEADERSHIP LESSONS 171

DAY 35. There is Room on the Mountain
for Climbers and Guides 173

DAY 36. Leadership Is Disappointing People 177

DAY 37. Even Good Soldiers Sometimes Die 181

DAY 38. The Moral Authority of Leadership 185

PART X. TEAMWORK 191

DAY 39. Build the Plan with Your Customer 193

DAY 40. F.A.T.T. 197

INTRODUCTION

I wonder what the term "business leader" conjures up for you.

If I had to take a wild stab, I would imagine the first thing that came to mind was a laundry list of duties. The job description. The day-to-day responsibilities that keep your business running and thriving.

And you wouldn't be wrong. Running or managing a business requires action.

But I'd like to expand your mind a bit.

Business is similar to a switchboard—but instead of distributing electrical power to other circuits, a business leader imparts power to people.

This may sound like an odd analogy. Bear with me.

As a leader in business, you are a power center, an apparatus with many functions and responsibilities. Others depend on you for vision, empowerment, support, and growth. You are a conduit for feeding life into others. A people-centered business leader sees the importance of the whole machine—that it cannot run without engaging every gear and every cog—but you are the powerhouse that keeps the wheels turning.

But your power has to come from somewhere, too. You can't give power that you don't have.

So, this is where you become set apart, you're not just the manager of a money-making machine.

Your power doesn't come from an electric current. Your power comes from a different Source—the power of God working in you and through you.

Many of us don't really think about business leadership as an incubator for producing a life of Kingdom purpose, mobilizing people to live and share Kingdom values. Many of us don't really think about business as a ministry. But friends, that's exactly what it is. If you are a business leader, you have a ministry.

Absent of business as a God-given commission, business is just . . . business. It's managing employees. It's making big decisions. It's setting and accomplishing lofty goals. It's monitoring team performance.

Is that enough for you?

I think He wants more for you.

It is my deepest desire that this short devotional will change the way you think about and do business. The secret sauce to a rewarding Kingdom business is in the people you impact—your clients and your team. As you run your business with Kingdom values, your people will become conduits of your Kingdom purpose.

And there's a bonus.

It's not just your business that will profit from a heart of service. It will overflow into every area of your life outside of the workplace.

People will sharpen your double-edged sword—a prosperous business and a rewarding life.

Wield it.

Connect and subscribe to get weekly leadership lessons at www.leadershipworthliving.com.

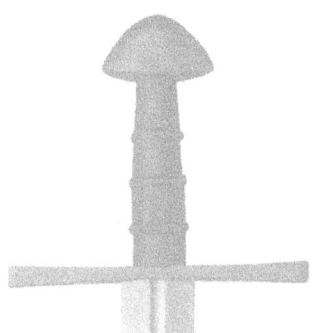

PART 1
ACHIEVING SUCCESS IN BUSINESS

DAY 1

THE BIRTHPLACE OF GREAT IDEAS

Great ideas come from a good idea. In fact, they come from refining and combining *multiple* good ideas.

What do you do with your good ideas? Do you write them down?

A couple of years ago, I was trying to solve a problem. We often run marketing campaigns at the very beginning of the month, and because automotive incentives are continually changing at the end of each month, we are often unable to send the new offer in print and mail it out on time for the events we run the first week of a month. This is an even more challenging task at the start of a year.

So I began to think and write down my ideas in the form of questions:

What if we posted the offers online so we could change or update them as the programs change? Good idea #1.

Then I thought, *what if the website was so interactive that customers could build their own offers online?* Good idea #2.

And, *what if the mail piece was so clean and simple that all it did was say "go online," but it was classy enough that people would take it seriously?* Good idea #3.

And, *what if the event had a name that was intriguing, so much so that customers would be exceptionally curious about the offer?* Good idea #4.

And lastly, *how can we make the mailed envelope with the invitation jump out of the mail so people will open it?* Good idea #5.

YOU AREN'T STUCK BECAUSE OF A LACK OF IDEAS—YOU'RE STUCK BECAUSE THEY HAVEN'T BEEN REFINED AND COMBINED.

Here's what came of it.

Good idea #1 became a dynamic website where we could easily upload new offers and change them on the fly.

Good idea #2 became a series of checkboxes online where a customer could choose the offers they wanted.

Good idea #3 became a laminated card.

Good idea #4 became an event with the catchy name "The Irresistible Offer."

Good idea #5 became a black envelope.

This became our most successful January event ever, and the response and sales were a direct reflection of that success.

You aren't stuck because of a lack of ideas—you're stuck because they haven't been refined and combined.

So rather than sit on your good ideas, write them down, and turn several good ideas into one great idea!

DAY 2

MOMENTUM HAS A FRIEND NAMED DISCIPLINE

Momentum is a beautiful thing. Many have compared it to a freight train on a rusty track; it takes a tremendous amount of energy to get it moving, but once it's moving, it can plow through just about anything.

When you have it—by ALL means—work hard to sustain it.

The problem with momentum is that it often comes with a cost. Momentum can cover up so many weaknesses in your products and services.

Let's first review the power of momentum. It can carry you even if your product or service isn't perfect (I call this market momentum). Sometimes market momentum can come from years of hard work, capitalizing on good ideas, or being in the right place at the right time with the right solution. If you are wise, you will leverage the momentum and never stop tweaking and improving your product and service offerings.

Paradoxically, the success momentum produces can end up being your biggest challenge. Here's what I mean by this: Momentum can have you running so hard just to keep up with demand and to scale your business that before you know it, your organization is stretched too thin.

So, to sustain momentum, you must leverage it with discipline. Develop the habits to shift the relentless pursuit of more business and more success to a relentless pursuit of innovation and excellence without saying "yes" to everything.

> **YOU CAN RIDE THE WAVE OF MOMENTUM AND STILL LACK THE DISCIPLINE TO FIGHT THE BATTLE OF EXCELLENCE.**

This, my friend, is very, very hard to do.

It's especially hard when you are coming from virtually nothing and struggling to survive, because then, when you have your first taste of success that comes from momentum, it appears you can suddenly do no wrong.

But you can do wrong. You can ride the wave of momentum and still lack the discipline to fight the battle of excellence.

Discipline doesn't just involve saying "yes."

It also involves knowing when to say "no" to seemingly boundless opportunities.

DAY 3

WALKING ON THE EDGE

One time, I was with a friend in Guatemala, and we were discussing the topic of taking risks as an entrepreneur, including my willingness to "risk it all" for something I can sense and at times, taste—but can't quite see.

In this conversation, I shared one of the biggest struggles I face as an entrepreneur: A few members of senior leadership are more risk-averse than I am, and I have to be intentional in regularly sharing with them what I see and sense so that they are emotionally able to support me. They lean more towards security and towards protecting the company, and at times, they may feel they need to protect the company from my drive.

My friend then replied with something that was very impactful to me. He said, "the view is clearer when you are walking on the edge." How true that is!

WHEN WE CAN FEEL THE PROBLEM, WE ARE CLOSER TO SEEING THE SOLUTION.

As entrepreneurs, especially visionary entrepreneurs, we are driven by a burning desire to make something better, to fix something we see as a problem, or to maximize an opportunity. We see something that we believe we can change. But we have to keep our team in mind without compromising on our drive.

You may be an edge walker, but your team may be guardrails. Your guardrails will be strongest when they see and understand your vision, so let them into your head a little bit—help them see what you see. This may alleviate some of the pushback that smothers your drive, and it may empower them to get on board.

So, what does it mean to walk on the edge? Walking on the edge can take on many shapes and sizes. Sometimes it's a financial edge as we push our resources to invent or re-invent (though I'm not advocating for prolonged financial stress). Other times, walking on the edge means that we are staying close enough to the problem so that we can discover clues that will lead us to the solution. When we can feel the problem, we are closer to seeing the solution.

The view is clearer when you walk on the edge.

DAY 4

WORSHIPPING SUCCESS JEOPARDIZES SUCCESS

There's really no shame in saying it....
Leaders want success.
The pursuit of success is virtuous. It is admirable. It is noble. But it is not meant to be worshipped. The second your climb to success becomes an idol, taking up most of the real estate in your brain, you may have a problem on your hands. The worship of success could be the very thing that keeps you *from* it.

YOU'LL KNOW YOU'RE SUCCESSFUL WHEN YOU ARE GROWING, NOT WHEN YOU ARRIVE.

The good news is success doesn't have to take a backseat. It may be your definition of success that needs a bit of an adjustment. When your definition of success is modified to accommodate your most valuable capital—people—your approach to obtaining that success will change... and so will your business. For the better. The pursuit of success is only as successful as your idea of what success entails.

Often, leaders struggle, fight, and constantly push uphill in the name of success. Any semblance of victory warrants celebration, and celebration is integral to endurance and comradery.

However, a long season of celebration may actually masquerade as an "arrival". "I've arrived" denotes completion, while "I'm on my way" denotes a humble acceptance of the need for perpetual growth. It's tough to worship success when you recognize: 1) you can't "arrive" there and 2) it is a work in progress. When you place a higher premium on progress, you weaken your fixation on the outcome.

You'll know you're successful when you are growing, not when you arrive. You should always work towards improvement.

Here's a reality check. Success isn't static. The economy doesn't stand still, nor does the market, nor does your competition. If you ever think your business is bullet proof then you probably have a blind spot, and it could be fatal.

I'm not advocating for paranoia, skepticism, or looking for problems. A cynical perspective isn't likely to create success. What I'm advocating for is humility.

Be humble, be willing to tweak your approach, and remember—worshipping success does not produce lasting success.

TAKEAWAY

What ideas are you squirreling away and how could you begin to release them? How well do you follow up the momentum you gain with action? How successful have you been in seeing the action to completion? What kind of changes do you notice when you "walk on the edge"? If someone were to ask you about your definition of success, what would you say? Are your priorities aligning with that definition?

WORSHIPPING SUCCESS JEOPARDIZES SUCCESS

PART 2
ENGAGING PEOPLE IN BUSINESS

DAY 5

YOUR HEART IS MEANT TO BE SHARED

You can lead, you can build a business, and you can generate revenue. This is a great start to effective leadership. But what connects a follower to a leader is their humanity. What makes a follower follow not only comes from their trust in the leader's business acumen and skillset but their trust in the leader's heart.

Think about the person in your life whom you trust the most. Why do you trust them? Would you trust them if you didn't know anything about them? Who they really are? Their desires, their dreams, their losses, their pain?

Can you build a meaningful relationship—personal or business—with someone you don't really know?

OTHERS WILL TRUST YOU WHEN YOU DEMONSTRATE THAT YOU TRUST THEM WITH YOUR HEART.

I was reading a business book by one of the greatest management consultants and authors of the last several decades, and in the book, he shared a personal story about his wife's battle with cancer. He then used a part of that story to draw a parallel lesson for business.

In some ways, it was a very simple analogy—and the business parallel made sense—but it wasn't the parallel that drew me in.

It was the story itself. I knew I was no longer dealing with just an expert. I was dealing with a person. A person whose success in business stemmed from a life laced with deep personal pain. It connected me to him, and quite frankly—it generated credibility.

Traditionally, business logic tells us to avoid the personal, to keep lessons objective—but just like any relationship, people listen more deeply and more closely to those who have allowed you to listen to them. Others will trust you when you demonstrate that you trust them with your heart. Head knowledge can intrigue but heart knowledge will mobilize people to action because they, too, have faced many struggles. People respond to relatability.

So, consider challenging the conventional paradigm of business as usual. A good businessman may know how to build a successful team, but your personal story will touch their hearts and foster richer connections.

When you talk to and lead others, always add "a touch of humanity" in the stories you share and the lessons you learn.

DAY 6

BEWARE OF THE WATER SKI EFFECT

Y ou may be the leader of a large, rapidly growing organization, or you may be a leader of a smaller organization who is actively working towards expansion.

The size of your organization doesn't really matter.

Either way, the decisions you make don't impact just one or two people; they impact many—and have a compounding effect.

For example, imagine that you are driving a power boat, and you have a water skier behind you.

What happens when you change direction? That water skier does a big fan out! He takes that corner far wider than you do. Your skier has to make ten times the adjustments that you do. What's more, you have prior knowledge of the turn. You can better and more quickly adapt because you know the move you are about to make. The water skier, on the other hand, is not afforded that luxury. They depend on your signal to properly prepare and respond to sudden change.

So, the little movements you make—the shifts in plans and the changes you make as a leader—can cause a tremendous wake to the people who are following you.

A GOOD LEADER LEADS TEAMS WHO WANT TO FOLLOW HIM, BUT THEY CAN'T FOLLOW YOU IF THEY CAN'T KEEP PACE WITH YOU.

I call it the water ski effect.

There's a natural order to changing course. Change, by its very nature, causes disruption, and is inevitable. You're going to have to make them. But change without warning can cause destruction.

So if you could maximize change by changing *with* your team, would you?

The wake caused by change can either be tumultuous or a gentle transfer of weight from one body part to the other.

Communicate your intention to shift gears ahead of time—"Hey, I'm about to turn"—so your team is prepared to take that corner. Help them understand *why* the boat needs to turn. Get them on board. If your team is not prepared, things likely won't go as planned, and you might have a little accident.

Be intentional with the decisions and changes you make, be intentional about communicating them to the team, and be intentional about not making changes too quickly.

A good leader leads teams who want to follow him. But if they can't keep pace with you, they can't follow you.

DAY 7

LENDING YOUR BELIEF

I remember talking with a friend of mine a while back about a popular book. The book was about pursuing and accomplishing your dreams. This friend said that while it was a very good book, it wasn't particularly helpful for 80% of its target audience.

My friend observed that the book was asking people this question: how do you turn your dream into reality? The problem with this question is: if 80% of people don't have a dream, how can they follow it?

Our conversation eventually led us to the power of "belief". You see, belief is the seed of a dream.

BELIEF IS THE SEED OF A DREAM.

So that's good news, because people who believe that they can accomplish something usually find a dream to accomplish.

So, it's very simple: The only missing piece to unlocking a dream is belief. That's the key!

There is one remaining problem, though. Many people who lack a dream also lack belief. They often go hand-in-hand.

If a person doesn't have a dream, and doesn't have belief, then you have to help them believe. So how can you do that?

You can lend them your belief. You start by sharing your beliefs and dreams with them.

Then, you invite them to come alongside you as you pursue your dreams.

As they work with you and see your dreams come true, they will be inspired and begin to believe in their own abilities and potential.

You tell them what a difference they are making in your life and what a difference they make in others' lives, and you intentionally encourage them with praise about the value they are adding to you. And be specific, not general—rather than just affirm *that* they offer value, specify *how* they offer value!

So, the lesson is this: Reach down, engage people in your dreams, and lend your belief to them.

Chances are, someone did the same for you.

DAY 8

FIND OUT WHAT THEY KNOW

Several years ago, a mentor of mine gave me an astute piece of advice.

"You already know what you know. Find out what they know."

To this day, this has served as one of the most valuable, powerful concepts in my personal life and business today. In fact, I now pause before every major meeting and ask myself, "Am I finding out what they know, or am I telling them what I know?"

You see, we are often eager to showcase what we know and how smart we are, especially if we are keen on impressing someone or earning their business or approval.

EVEN IF WE KNOW OUR PRODUCTS AND SOLUTIONS ARE RIGHT FOR THEM, WE NEED TO LEAD WITH QUESTIONS.

There are a few problems if you take the "here's what I know" approach to relationships and business:

First, what we share may not be as revolutionary as we think it is and consequently, we could lose credibility.

Second, we are assuming we know what they need from us, but what they need isn't always that simple.

Third, we can get "on a roll" selling, which puts us at risk of telling more than we need to. Instead, it is wise to share only part of what we know so that we have more to bring back later.

Even if we know our products and solutions are right for them, we need to lead with questions. Doing so gives us the context we need to present our solutions in a way that solves their *real* problems, not what we perceive their problems *to be*.

More importantly, true, effective leaders always lead with questions. They dialogue. They are more interested in perpetually seeking to understand their client's needs than telling the client what their needs are. This approach will position you as a trusted solution provider.

Indeed, questions build trust. When you ask your clients questions, they will see your genuine interest in their needs and willingness to customize your solutions to align with their perspectives and goals.

It's true that we must sell product.

But trust is always the first sale you need to make if you desire to build a long-term relationship.

TAKEAWAY

What does your team know about your personal story? What kind of disruption and discord have you noticed when your team is unprepared for changes that you make? What do you do when you notice a team member who is burdened by doubt and unbelief? What have you learned or what can you learn from others who are less experienced or seasoned than you?

_____
_____
_____
_____
_____
_____
_____
_____
_____
_____
_____
_____
_____
_____
_____
_____

THE DOUBLE-EDGED SWORD

PART 3
FAITH IN BUSINESS

PART 3

FAITH IN BUSINESS

DAY 9

GOD WILL FIND YOU EVERY TIME

Have you ever run yourself ragged to find peace when it seems to have run out? Does "I have tried everything I can, and I am still deeply entrenched in darkness, in pain, in hopelessness" sound vaguely familiar?

Sometimes, trying is the *problem*, not the solution. We become too focused on *doing* and not focused enough on *resting*. Because when you realize that we have a God who searches for us, yearns for us, and refuses to give up on us, we understand that we have been missing it—God has been looking for you all along, and your only marching order was to let yourself be found.

A few years ago, I went to mass at the Monastery where twenty-seven years before I had studied to become a Catholic Priest.

I walked the grounds after mass, and while walking the grounds, I met a monk, Brother Andrew, and we struck up a conversation. He asked me where I went to church, and I explained that I was a businessman with four children and was currently attending a Protestant church. I shared that I had attended the seminary at that Monastery twenty-seven years prior—the very year that he joined. He looked vaguely familiar. After our brief exchange, we parted ways, but before we did, Brother Andrew paused, looked at me, smiled, and said "God finds us."

TOO OFTEN WE PLACE OUR EYES ON OTHER THINGS AND WE MISS HIM.

Little did I know that the very next day I would start the journey of losing my biggest personal dream and that the next twelve months would be some of the hardest of my life. But no matter how tough or crazy life would get, when I would look to Him, God was there. The monk's words reverberated in my mind—God finds me.

God finds us, my friends.... He isn't just with us, He *finds* us. He is active, not passive. One might even say that He *pursues* us. Too often we place our eyes on other things and we miss Him. Yet if we would just look to Him, we would find that He is there, right by our sides, ready and eager to take us by the hand as we walk with Him and become part of the story He has already written for us.

DAY 10

RELATIONSHIP WITH GOD IS NOT THE END GOAL

So often in Christian circles, we talk about and emphasize having a relationship with God. But we rarely talk about intimacy with God. Perhaps that is because in Western Culture we aren't comfortable with the concept of intimacy. Intimacy is the very thing that is lacking in our families, our friendships, and our marriages.

So, what does it mean to be intimate with God and how does it differ from relationship with God?

Throughout our lives, we find ourselves in relationships with many different people—friends, spouses, children, colleagues, etc. But not every relationship has intimacy. They are not mutually inclusive. To be fair, not every relationship calls for intimacy, either. Intimacy may actually be harmful to us in certain relationships, such as your relationship with your boss.

God is the only exception to this rule. As Kingdom people, we need both—a relationship totally defined by intimacy.

Unfortunately, we often get in our own way while God is waving us down to come to Him with everything—including our transgressions and deepest areas of brokenness.

We already believe that He knows everything about us, so why do we try and hide things from Him?

Think about Adam and Eve. Their first response to their disobedience was to hide their faces from God in the Garden of Eden after eating the forbidden fruit. Not surprisingly, this wasn't successful. We can't hide from Him, and while at first blush that may sound discouraging, it's actually one of the most encouraging truths to ever grace our lives.

IF WE LET FEAR KEEP US FROM INTIMACY, THEN WE ARE LETTING FEAR KEEP US FROM GOD.

Maybe it's because we don't trust God? Maybe it's because we think we know what's best for us, and we don't want to lose control of our lives (despite the sobering truth that we don't have much control, in many respects)? Maybe it's because we have an "I've done my Christian duty for the day" checklist—prayers said, good deeds done, worship offered... CHECK!

Intimacy doesn't flow from a checklist or from duty, it only flows from love. We do our duty or follow a checklist from fear of consequences, not from love.

If we let fear keep us from intimacy, then we are letting fear keep us from God.

Walk with God today, not because we should, but because we can. Walk with God simply because you love Him.

DAY 11

DELIGHT BEGETS BLESSING

On Day 9, we talked about God's call for us to rest in Him because of the promise He has already given us—that He will find us in the middle of the greatest storms in our lives. Rather than trying to escape your pain, we are to rest in the glory of God's presence and persistent pursual of us in the thick of the pain.

Similarly, our efforts do not automatically elicit blessings from God.

ARE WE SO FOCUSED ON ACHIEVEMENT AND DOING, THAT WE THINK WE CAN BUY GOD'S BLESSING WITH GOOD BEHAVIOR?

God's blessings come solely from our faith in Him. They find us because He loves us. They show up because He already made the decision before the foundations of the earth to give us all things in spite of the defects that come with being a human being living in a broken world.

Some time ago, my friend spoke about living a life that is "bless-able"—a life that is fully in line with God's will. God's will is simple: to live a life that is pure and honoring to Him—loving Him and loving others.

That's it! End of story!

Indeed, that is all we need. To live a life that God's blessings can flow through. Too often in Western Christianity, we see God as a Santa Claus who makes our wishes come true if we are good. Are we so focused on achievement and doing, that we really think we can buy God's blessing with good behavior?

This thinking will entangle us in a life that is wrought with legalism, rules, and regulations, the very things that Jesus Christ came to free us from. Why would we choose a life of bondage over a life of freedom?

The Bible urges us to "delight yourself in the Lord and He will give you the desires of your heart" (Psalm 37:4). What does it mean to delight in the Lord? When I think of the word delight, I think of childlike joy, a simple, pure happiness; a state where my "soul is smiling." When I delight in a relationship, I am in unity with someone with whom I share a mutual joy that seems to bounce between our hearts.

Delight in God, feel His love surround you today, be joyful in His love, and delight in Him; and yes, perhaps then, your heart will align with His, and His blessings will flow through your life.

DAY 12

DARE TO DIE THE SECOND DEATH

Generally, death carries with it an unpleasant sense of dread—something to be avoided, not embraced. We typically avoid the topic.

The fallacy of this way of thinking is that death is the precursor to life. We see the evidence of this everywhere we look. All of God's creation is sustained through the cycles of death and life. All seed-bearing plants die to make room for new fruit-bearing life. Every living creature must die to accommodate a balanced ecosystem.

We aren't that much different. But for us, the death that bears much fruit is spiritual death.

I was with a friend of mine at a retreat in a beautiful lodge in New Zealand. While we were enjoying all there is to enjoy about such a magnificent place, he looked at me and said: "What lies beyond significance?" We talked about what that was, and my answer to him was, "It's insignificance."

I was referring to a conversation I had the year before when I talked with a large ministry leader about "the first and second deaths".

PERHAPS HE ALSO LOOKS FOR PEOPLE WHO WILL DIE A SECOND DEATH.

On the journey to success, there comes a point where we can decide if our lives will be primarily about ourselves or about others. It's at that point where we can choose to either stay on the success journey or take a deeper, more meaningful path to significance, which is found by defining ourselves predominantly by the value we add to others, rather than the trophies, influence, or positions we achieve for ourselves.

This is the first death, where we die to chasing success for ourselves, and instead pursue significance as we begin to measure our life by what we give.

But there is a second death. This is where we die to identifying ourselves and our worth by what we give to others. We stop pursuing even charitable awards and philanthropic recognition. Instead, we say "it's no longer about me, it's about God." Let's give Him the glory. Wow, if we could realize just how insignificant we are ... we would truly realize how significant God is. It's all about Him.

I do believe that God looks for successful people He can trust to influence society as salt and light who will help bring His Kingdom to earth.

But perhaps that isn't all. Perhaps He also looks for people who will die a second death to their own ego-driven identity, people He might use in ways that we can't even begin to comprehend.

DAY 13

LETTING GO DOESN'T MEAN GIVING UP

I think I speak on behalf of everyone when I say that waiting is one of the most painstaking mainstays we have to endure throughout the entirety of our lives.

If you really think about it, we are always waiting for something. The act of waiting is a staple in our lives—in every season.

I'm convinced that delay is not the enemy. In reality, the true enemy is really our perception of delay. Delay gives us something. It doesn't take away.

When we are on God's timetable, we are always being given something. God's timing is a form of protection. If we are still waiting for something from God, it's because receiving it today could actually lead to destruction—either our own or someone else's.

I once read a book by an author who has a tremendous gift of faith. He said that faith has to do with the invisible, and patience has to do with timing.

Our hopes and dreams aren't always fulfilled on our watch, and we can become discouraged when the clock continues to tick as we remain empty-handed. At times, we feel in our soul that perhaps we need to let go of something, but we are hesitant to let go, because we don't want to give up faith.

LETTING GO DOESN'T MEAN GIVING UP. IT MAY JUST MEAN GIVING IT OVER.

Yet we still can't shake that voice telling us to let go.

Letting go doesn't mean giving up. It may just mean giving it over.

Giving it over can be an even greater act of faith. Perhaps it's our way of saying to God, "You put this desire on my heart, now I will give it back to you because I trust you."

As humans, we are naturally impatient. We want our dreams and goals to come to fruition today. Waiting on God, as hard as it can be, is an act of worship.

Faith secures the promise, but patience allows God to give it to us at the right time.

As humans, we want to "make things happen" in *our* time. Maybe God is telling us to hand it over to Him and trust that He will give it back to us at the *right* time.

TAKEAWAY

Can you think of a time in your life when you have been "found" by God? In what ways has your relationship with God evolved into intimacy? At what points in your life have you felt God blessed you the most, and how were you pursuing God at the time? What kind of challenges have you faced when setting aside your own self-imposed identity? What is your kneejerk reaction to giving your plans over to God?

PART 4
GENEROSITY IN BUSINESS

DAY 14

GIVING STARTS THE FLOW

I want to share a story that I believe will help add tremendous value to your life and your organization. So much of our return on investment comes from how much we invest in the world around us—in others' lives and in their stories.

In a mentoring session with Dr. John C. Maxwell, I asked him what he saw in me that was unique. He replied:

"Jeff, you are generous, exceptionally generous, but there are several things about your generosity that stand out. First, you have a passion not only to give but to engage others in giving, to inspire them to give, and to join you."

> **GIVING INVOLVES WILLINGNESS AND EAGERNESS TO GET YOUR HANDS DIRTY TO REALLY IMPACT THE ORGANIZATIONS YOU GIVE TO.**

"Secondly, you really believe that your giving makes a difference, and that belief gives you authority. Lots of people give and want to make a difference, but they often don't believe they will. You do."

Thirdly, most people who give tend to give out of overflow, but you give to get the flow."

I have since thought about these a fair bit and now understand two things:

1) Generosity is so much more than giving money; it is getting involved. Giving involves willingness and eagerness to get your hands dirty to really impact the organizations you give to. Only then will you see the return and experience the return.

2) Generosity is bringing others on the journey with you and watching their lives transform as they begin their own journey of giving. This is the greatest joy of giving and is the reason why I refuse to simply give out of the overflow. That's easy to do.

No, I give to get the flow, because giving is an investment. I want to be a river, not a dam. I want to be a conduit, so more blessings can flow through me to those I partner with. I want to give before I have determined whether I have enough *to* give. You can never outgive God. Abundance comes in when abundance goes out.

Here it is: if you want to have significance in your life, give generously, bring other people with you, get involved, and give to get the flow.

DAY 15

QUESTIONS TO GUIDE YOUR GIVING

As compassionate entrepreneurs, there is one challenge we face that isn't often addressed.

Other organizations will hear through the grapevine that you have a reputation and passion for liberal giving. Make no mistake—this is a *good* thing. I don't know about you, but if there was anything I want to be known for, it's that I live a life of devotion to serving others.

A COMPASSIONATE ENTREPRENEUR IS A RELATIVELY RARE COMMODITY, AND YOU WILL BE PRESENTED WITH OPPORTUNITIES TO GIVE... ALMOST DAILY.

Where the challenge comes in is making the important decision on where to invest your time, money, and energy when there are an overwhelmingly large number of organizations whose causes are changing the world and building the Kingdom. Many voices will clamor for your attention and make bids for your help, usually because they are seeking partnerships with those who build for the sake of equipping others to build. Every organization wants this—as they should!

So, a compassionate entrepreneur is a relatively rare commodity, and you will be presented with opportunities to give ... almost daily.

One day, Dr. John C. Maxwell talked with a group of us about how he decides to give, where he decides to give, and why he decides to give to where he has decided to give. John encouraged us to answer five questions when presented with opportunities that will help determine where to give:

1) The first is the <u>leadership question</u>. Does the leadership of the organization have the character and capacity to effectively steward your gift?
2) The second is the <u>return question</u>. What is the return or ROI that the work of this organization delivers? What are their measurable output and outcomes?

3) The third question is the <u>involvement question</u>. Can I give more than money? Are they asking for my input and thoughts, will they welcome it, or do they really just want a check?
4) The fourth is the <u>personal question</u>. Is this an organization that I have a personal desire to support based on a friendship or relationship, personal experience, or my own life's journey?
5) The fifth is the <u>nudge question</u>. Do I personally feel that God is nudging me to support this organization, perhaps for a purpose bigger than or outside of my personal preferences?

You do not have to give to everything and everyone. There is an organization that needs something from you that only you can give. Give there.

DAY 16

THE SECRET BEHIND THE SECRET

Success is multilayered. Just when we think we have found the secret formula to driving results and impact, we soon encounter another as we dig a little deeper.

But really, the core of our success always boils down to one thing–our hearts.

Jesus speaks to this when he says, "For where your treasure is, there your heart will be also" (Matthew 6:21).

Here's the thing about the treasure of our hearts: It determines our treasure in the natural.

I was with one of my automotive trainers in France and we were discussing the astounding results from our clients that come out of our businesses, and how the success seems to flow out of our passion, our belief, and our positive expectations.

But even passion, beliefs, thinking, and expectation have a source. Without that source, these things are fragile, shakable, and temporal. There is a foundation upon which those things are built; otherwise, the bottom would fall out.

> **IF OUR SOUL IS DEEPLY ROOTED IN GRATITUDE FOR WHO WE ARE AND WHAT WE HAVE BEEN GIVEN, OUR LIFE AUTOMATICALLY ORIENTS AROUND POSITIVE EXPECTATION.**

During this discussion with my trainer, I expressed how grateful I was for the opportunity to expand my business into France.

He responded with something so tremendously impactful. He said, "Gratitude is the secret behind the secret."

Many people think that the secret to success comes from positive thinking or positive expectation. Indeed, those things both help to create success because they positively frame our outlook.

But there is something much more influential to success than our mental condition. It's the spirit with which we approach life. It's the condition of our soul.

If our soul is deeply rooted in gratitude for who we are and what we have been given, our life automatically orients around positive expectation; but even more, we naturally seek to serve, add value to others, and be a life-giver. This spirit, or condition of the soul, isn't just an additional ingredient for success—it is the adhesive holding every virtuous element of your character together.

Yes, the secret to a fruitful business, and more specifically and importantly, a fruitful life, is found in your thoughts. But the secret to that secret is a deeply rooted spirit of gratitude.

TAKEAWAY

How do you determine when to give and how to give? What kind of experiences have you had with giving when it felt like there wasn't much to give? What kind of experiences have you had with giving from a place of abundance? Have you ever questioned a decision you made in giving to a specific cause? What do you think contributed to that discomfort? What do you have to be grateful for today?

THE SECRET BEHIND THE SECRET

PART 5
GROWTH IN BUSINESS

DAY 17

PEOPLE BEFORE PRODUCTION

Growth requires a sophisticated understanding of the interaction between people and production.

First, take a moment to answer some key questions:

What is it that you value the most?

Are you a "get things done," almost at any cost, production, performance, and results kind of person?

Are you growth-driven?

Do you have aggressively ambitious dreams and goals to grow your company?

What kind of business are you in? Do short-term results drive your thinking and operations because you are in a short-cycle business (like the automotive business)?

We all know that there is truth in the leadership cliché: "all production comes from people," and that long-term, we need to develop people so they can produce more—it's not a "chicken and the egg" scenario.

YOU MAY NEED TO INVEST IN YOUR CURRENT TEAM AND BUSINESS FIRST.

We also know, assuming your company can run with its current team at status quo, you need to invest before you grow... either in training existing people or in hiring new people.

But before we get too philosophical, you need to answer one of the most important questions:

Can your company really run effectively if your current team is operating at status quo?

As businesspeople, we all like to talk, plan, and dream of growth, and some of us have been blessed with high growth seasons in business.

But can your existing team function with the business it already has with minimal stress 85% of the time? 90% of the time?

It's all too easy to convince ourselves that we are ready to grow our business, when in reality many aspects of our operations are currently being held together by short term "band-aid" style solutions.

Take a breath, put off your next strategizing, goal-setting, or planning session for at least a week and analyze your business with the 85% rule.

You may need to invest in your current team and business first.

And that is likely the best investment you can make.

DAY 18

TWO DEGREES AT A TIME

I was having dinner with a very wealthy businessman in New Zealand, and we were discussing business lessons.

He shared this thought with me: "Good businesses go bad two degrees at a time."

This is so true. It is the culmination of so many little things that can cause a business to go bad. Rarely does disaster strike because of one big event or one big decision.

Rather, the biggest crashes are the product of the smallest fender benders, and at the root of them all is . . .

The insidious traps of success.

THE MINUTE YOUR SUCCESS IS CELEBRATED MORE THAN YOUR CUSTOMER'S SUCCESS, YOU ARE HEADING SOUTH TWO DEGREES AT A TIME.

Success begets growth. If you add people who aren't the right fit or even add *good* people who are only 80% the right fit, but you don't take the time to show them the ethos of your organization's culture, the ways in which you think about the business, why you do what you do (and not just *how* you do it), then your culture will become diluted, and your business will start to nosedive two degrees at a time.

Success also begets a habit of saying "yes" to opportunities. Indeed, successful businessmen often pride themselves on "rising to an opportunity" or "being a hero" to their customers.

But too many "yeses" will stretch your resources and you will soon find yourself doing one hundred and forty projects with mediocrity rather than one hundred projects well.

You'll begin to measure your company's success by how many projects you complete, not by the excellence of each project, all because you said yes to too many opportunities.

Finally, success in an organization automatically creates an inward focus as you celebrate what your company achieves rather than what your customers achieve. The minute your success is celebrated more than your customer's success, you are heading south two degrees at a time.

Fiercely guard your culture, learn to say no to opportunities that will compromise your quality of delivery, and celebrate your customer's success more than your own.

Take it from me. These are mistakes I have made all too many times, and they have cost me dearly.

Be proactive and keep your business from going south two degrees at a time.

DAY 19

PUT EACH PROBLEM IN A BOX

Have you ever noticed that problems aren't always isolated events, but they seem to ebb and flow through the river of life—sometimes unexpectedly popping to the surface, and other times piling up in waves that it feels like they are holding our heads underwater?

Here's what I want to illustrate about problems:

If you spend your time counting them, calling them all by name, you will develop a relationship with all of them at one time. This is problematic, because just like you cannot possibly nurture every relationship in our lives with the same level of care, you cannot thoughtfully attend to every problem simultaneously. Just like you can end up with a lot of shallow relationships if you are spread too thin, your problems will be patched up like amateur stitchwork if you try to tackle them all at once.

There's a better way.

AND, BOXING OUR PROBLEMS AND UNBOXING THEM ONE AT A TIME SOUNDS SIMPLE. WHILE IT MAY NOT BE A COMPLICATED CONCEPT, IT'S ALSO NOT EASY.

I was talking with a very good friend about how, at times, my life seems like one never-ending battle after another. I want to improve virtually every area of my life. But some of the challenges are harder to tackle than others. Each problem seems to require so much of my energy and efforts. When I try to engage with all of them, I get discouraged.

We weren't built for this kind of capacity.

With great wisdom, my friend advised me to "put each problem in a box and solve one problem at a time." Wow, it sounds so simple.

And, boxing our problems and unboxing them one at a time *sounds* simple. While it may not be a complicated concept, it's also not easy.

I proceeded to write down my top six challenges, each representing its own box. Then, I began to define three action steps I could take for each box. I then wrote down the top six areas where I wanted to see positive change and noted two

PUT EACH PROBLEM IN A BOX

action steps for each box. I then prioritized the boxes. Next, I started with one box, solved it, opened a second box, and solved that one. A few days later, I opened the third box. I was also surprised at the peace I gained knowing that I didn't have to open every box... yet!

Put your problems in a box and solve them one box at a time.

DAY 20

WE ARE ASKING THE WRONG QUESTION

On Day 13, we talked about God's timing and how the depth of our impatient hearts is exposed when we are at His mercy.

Just like children nestled in the back seat of a car on a family trip prod their parents with the irksome question, "Are we there yet?", we too find ourselves asking the question:

"How long will it take?"

See, we are no different than young children. Our favorite word is "when".

But this question often breeds a disappointing answer—either one we don't want or the absence of one.

There's another question that better serves us....

..."How far can I go?"

HOW VALUABLE IS FINISHING IF WE LEARNED NOTHING?

The question, "How long will it take?" is fraught with impatience. It implies that you have somewhere to go that's more important, and where you are now is a nuisance that is holding you up. In a world that seems to value only progress and measures worth based on productivity, it's a natural question to ask. We want to complete a project, check off a box, and move on to something newer, bigger, and better. The challenge with focusing on the speed with which we can complete something or move past something is that we often don't stop long enough to take a step back and learn from where we are.

When we are in a hurry, we miss growth opportunities that could be game changers for prospering us in that very place we are so eager to arrive at.

It's the difference between being growth-oriented rather than goal-oriented.

Eventually, we will finish what we are seeking to finish. But how valuable is finishing if we learned nothing? Could we have been more equipped for our future assignment had we sunk our teeth into our present?

The next time you hear yourself asking, "How long will this take?", pause and reconsider whether you are asking yourself the right question.

DAY 21

BUILD THROUGH IT TO GET THROUGH IT

How do you respond to the wrenches that are thrown in your plans?

When life gets stormy, most people make the mistake of just trying to get through their problems. The more daunting and formidable the problem, the greater the desire to remove the problem.

What transpires is a fervent effort to just get the problem over with. There's such a distinct irony to this response, because the more effort we put into ending the problem, the more the problem tries to end us. It's a soul-sucking vortex that will drain you dry. Trying to outrun your problems is a losing battle. And sometimes, even just trying to survive takes a lot of work.

But that energy *could* be useful. It just needs to be redirected.

PROBLEMS HELP YOU BUILD. WITHOUT THEM, YOU CAN'T BUILD MUCH.

If we could take even 20% of that energy we put into getting through the problem and instead put it into learning from the problem, we probably wouldn't recognize ourselves even just a few short months down the road. In fact, our attitudes about hardship would change dramatically in such a way that the next time we encounter another wrench, we might actually use it for its intended purpose—as a tool.

If you have ever owned a toolbox, you'll understand how fitting the imagery of a tool is for grasping just how empowering your problems can be.

Take a hammer, for example. A hammer has power. There's a tremendous force behind it—it can literally drill a piece of steel into a block or plank of wood.

It isn't a victim. It tells the nail what to do, but it also does something great—it builds. It builds that home for that family. It builds that hospital. It builds that family business.

What does this have to do with our problems?

Problems help you build. Without them, you can't build much. Our problems are like the nail, and you are the hammer. Nails say to a hammer, "Here I am! Use me to build a strong house!" Problems say to you, "Here I am! Use me to build a strong life!"

Nails are worthless without a hammer, and hammers are worthless without a nail.

Be a hammer, not a nail.

TAKEAWAY

What kind of changes have you noticed take place when you prioritize people? When you prioritize your product? What does success mean to you? Who drives your objective to achieve success? How do you tackle your problems? How can you place each problem in its own box in the future? What is your attitude toward growth and learning, even if it means enduring misfortune? When you have tried to press the eject button instead of learning through it, and what was the result?

_____
_____
_____
_____
_____
_____
_____
_____
_____
_____
_____
_____
_____
_____

PART 6
HANDLING PEOPLE

DAY 22

EVERY DAY YOU ICE A TEAM

"I'll do A when I'm B."

"I'll invest in X when I've arrived at Y."

Have you ever noticed that humans tend to delay those action items that would lead to greater prosperity in their personal lives and businesses because it's "not the right time"?

We see this when we wait too long for circumstances to be just right—to have the right-sized team, with the right experience, with the right qualifications . . . and the list goes on.

It's not uncommon when you are selling training services, as we do at Absolute Results, that your clients will say, "I believe in training, but I don't have the right staff yet. . . . come see me in a few months once I have hired some new staff whom I know are right. Then I will invest in training them."

I remember when I first encountered this objection, I saw it like the "chicken and the egg" question: How can you grow a strong sales team unless you train them?

EVERY DAY AND EVERY HOUR THAT CUSTOMERS CALL, EMAIL, OR VISIT YOUR BUSINESS IS A GAME DAY WITH A PRIME OPPORTUNITY TO SCORE A GOAL.

Ultimately the best answer came from one of my clients.

He voiced who on his staff was successful and a keeper, whom he would likely lose, who had potential, and who he would likely let go. He then said, "Jeff, it's like a hockey farm team—it's far from perfect, I will always need to recruit, but every day, I need to ice a team."

He continued: "Every day is a game day, so I look at my team and assess, *who is on the bench? Who can I put on the ice and where? What are the team dynamics?* I position each shift or each crew with a veteran, a rookie, a closer, a relational salesperson, etc. so I can get the best results with the team I ice each and every game."

So, if you wait for the perfect team and only ice or invest in those whom you believe are long-term players, your business will suffer. But if you take the imperfect team, including the players on the bench, and find a way to put them on the ice, your business will prosper.

The lesson is this: Every day and every hour that customers call, email, or visit your business is a game day with a prime opportunity to score a goal.

Ice your team daily. Coach them and invest in them, or you will miss far too many shots at the net, and the opportunity cost of those missed shots will be great. Even worse, you might miss developing some players that, given the right opportunities to play, could rise up and elevate their game.

DAY 23

PUT A NUMBER ON THEIR HEAD

You don't need to be a leader in business to know that some people are just... harder to work with.

Maybe they are obstinate. Maybe they have a sour attitude. Or maybe it's something as simple as a lack of chemistry.

I want to impart a very personal technique for dealing with difficult people in your life.

You can't change people, and many of the most frustrating ones will be permanent figures in your life.

I want to share an effective way of managing and neutralizing your frustration.

Imagine an uncle who just seems to irritate you every time your paths intersect, no matter what you do or how hard you try to appease him.

Assign him a number between one and ten, with one representing severe relational limitations and ten representing no limitations or someone who is always a pleasure to engage. Let's pretend you assigned him a six.

YOU CAN'T EXPECT A TEN FROM A SIX.

According to your selected number, your uncle is simply a middle-of-the-road kind of guy who is doing the best he can. He has tremendous weaknesses.

But he also has notable strengths.

By associating character capacity with a numeric value, you neutralize the agitation you feel when you interact with that person bearing the value you assign. Simply remember, "that's how a six acts." Gradually, you will begin to accept him for who he is rather than who you want him to be.

By executing this technique, you can buffer yourself against disappointment from those in your life whom you wish could be tens but are really just sixes.

Lower your expectations. Put a number on that person's head. You can't expect a ten from a six.

Every once in a while, you may be pleasantly surprised when your six person behaves like a seven or an eight—a shift that you may not have seen if you remained resolved to holding them to a standard they simply could not meet.

DAY 24

NOT A SAVIOR, BUT A WALKER

Not too long ago, I had the opportunity to listen to an incredible transformation leader whose ministry has worked with thousands of former inmates, drug dealers, gang members, and criminals.

They are accredited with a 70% success rate in transforming peoples' lives—more than double that of any other organization in Los Angeles.

He didn't say their primary job was to "save people," or "do things for people."

He said their one and only objective was to "walk with people."

A WALKER BELIEVES IN A SUFFERING PERSON. A SAVIOR DOES NOT.

While this doesn't negate the power of the accomplishments of this organization, it *does* highlight the power of the human soul to overcome and "pull oneself up."

When you walk with people, you communicate, "I'll be by your side as you do this." When you attempt to save people, you communicate, "I'll change your circumstances so that you don't have to do what you're doing."

Not very empowering, is it?

Humans cannot save. What's more, a savior will rob someone of their confidence to overcome future hardship.

A walker believes in a suffering person. A savior does not.

And all it takes is just one person who believes in them and gives them the selfless gift of companionship.

His statement is a tribute to human resilience and the power of unconditional love.

It flies in the face of prejudice and ego-driven ministry that takes credit for someone else's victory, which robs that person of their dignity, and most importantly... God's glory.

When this ministry leader was asked why he gives people a "second chance", his reply was: "many of these people never had a first chance."

If we insist on trying to be rescuers and savers of people, we will miss the joy of witnessing true restoration of dignity. We will get in God's way, and we will burn out...

And become victims.

DAY 25

THE QUESTION THAT TURNS CRITICISM INTO A CLOSE

You can turn anything around that has been turned upside down.

I was in a meeting last week with the CEO of a large client. The meeting wasn't going very well; as a matter of fact, the CEO started the meeting attributing his failing business to my company, accusing us of very poor business practices.

Ironically, these were the very business practices many of his managers were guilty of and which I vigorously opposed.

After twenty minutes, the CEO summed up his position and then looked to me for my response. I thanked him for his candor, expressed that my company's goal was to add value to his businesses and if I hadn't, that was not my intent.

I then asked the question that would turn everything around: *"How and where can we add value to you?"*

ONE OF THE TOUGHEST MEETINGS IN MY PROFESSIONAL CAREER BECAME BOTH A LEARNING LESSON AND OPENED THE DOOR TO A NEW OPPORTUNITY.

I asked if he would allow me thirty minutes to give the presentation I had prepared.

Thirty minutes later, I summarized my presentation and asked which of the services I presented might fill a need or add value to his organization. We ended the meeting with two key projects to work on for his team.

One of the toughest meetings in my professional career became both a learning lesson and opened the door to a new opportunity.

Here's how I turned what looked like a bleak outcome for my business proposition into a client whose trust in me and my company had been restored:

1) I was prepared for the meeting because I knew his business and my business.

THE QUESTION THAT TURNS CRITICISM INTO A CLOSE

2) I had the emotional capacity to sit in front of a barrage of accusations and remain calm.
3) I sincerely desired to add value and I offered that value to him.

When you are backed into a corner and doors seem to be closing, ask your prospect how you can add value to them, and then put your energy into that task.

DAY 26

WHICH BATTLE WILL YOU LOSE?

Some battles are meant to be lost. Some losses actually serve you. But there's another that will wreck you.

Not long ago, I was with my friend Carlos, conversing about his new project to fight human trafficking. We discussed how that industry was controlled by organized crime and how dangerous it is to "walk into the devil's territory" and declare war.

Carlos then made a profound statement: "It's okay to lose a battle against the enemy, but don't lose a battle against fear."

Wow. Don't lose a battle against fear.

Fear itself is what we are fighting. Not the enemy that we fear.

Carlos is right. There are battles we will lose. "Lose the battle, but win the war", is a rather cliché statement, but is actually a profound concept.

Just like a football game, a team could lose a quarter and still end up taking the victory.

What holds you back from engaging in a battle, embracing a new challenge or opportunity, or making a risky step forward to reinvent or shift your business or ministry?

WHEN WE FEEL THERE IS SOMETHING WE NEED TO DO THAT IS THE *RIGHT* THING TO DO, BUT WE CONTINUE TO PAUSE, THAT'S FEAR.

I am not suggesting that you forge full speed ahead at the expense of wisdom. Sometimes it isn't fear holding us back, but a response to what you know could reap far-reaching consequences if not thought through.

So, fear and wisdom have something in common: They both incite pause, but one comes from a destructive source, and the other is driven by a constructive source.

For example, caution and logic often give us pause, and they should. But when we feel there is something we need to do that is the *right* thing to do, but we continue to pause, that's fear.

In business, the tough decisions aren't between right choices and wrong choices. They are between good choices and great choices. Don't let fear keep you from great choices.

Great choices are often the ones that you know are risky, but deep down inside your entrepreneurial heart, you also know they are right for your business and organization.

And most importantly, just because you lose the first quarter doesn't mean you made a wrong decision.

DAY 27

SURPRISE THEM WITH A THANK YOU

We all want to feel that we are important.

We all want to know that our efforts to protect our families, bless others in our workplace, honor God in our churches, and contribute to a greater purpose are not in vain.

We want to believe that what we do everyday matters.

But do we really believe it?

Do the people in your life know that you believe that about them?

We hear a lot about the importance of providing positive feedback to your team, but the importance of specific feedback has been quite understated.

WHEN YOU TAKE YOUR EYE FOR DETAIL AND EXTEND IT TO THEM, YOUR TEAM WILL FEEL CARED FOR, NOTICED, AND VALUED.

A powerful way to show honor to people on your team is to thank them for something specific they did that they were unaware was helpful.

How big or small is inconsequential—in fact, sometimes your gratitude for the smaller things may come as a much bigger surprise to them, because we don't often suspect that the small ways in which we serve could impact someone else in such big ways!

Your team notices your attention to detail. They've seen you at work.

When you take your eye for detail and extend it to them, your team will feel noticed and valued.

I remember when my mentor's CEO approached me at an event where they were training over 500 faith leaders from around the world. He told me to look around the room. He said, "all of this is because of you." I didn't understand what he meant, so I questioned him. He stated that I was one of three people who, over the last eighteen months, spoke vision, encouragement, and faith into my mentor at just the time he needed. It gave him confirmation and bolstered his faith. It gave him the strength to carry on.

There have been many times I have looked at leaders in the eyes and told them how much they mean to me, and how they have benefitted the organization. When I can point to something they did or a special word or action of theirs that I noticed (especially when they didn't realize how impactful their word or action was), I remember the most important reason why I am where I am:

My team.

TAKEAWAY

Who is sitting on your bench that may be waiting for some game time? What kind of expectations do you have for people you interact with? Do you find you often feel disappointed in those interactions? In what ways are you trying to save versus walk with someone in need? How do you respond to client rejection and how could you regain their respect? What battles are you afraid to lose? How could you surprise each of your team members with a "thank you" today?

PART 7
HIGHER THINKING

DAY 28

WILL YOU SURVIVE, STRIVE, OR THRIVE?

Take a moment right now to take inventory of your daily environment.

Who are you spending time with? Where do you go? What do you spend your time doing?

Now, answer these questions: Whom have you become as a result? Who were you before?

Most likely, you are different now than you were then simply because your social circles, daily activities, and interests are different.

Because we are products of our environment, we need to be intentional about the environments that we are creating. The same principle applies to the organizations we lead. How you work will create the environment you lead.

So, I ask you: are you surviving, striving, or thriving?

Because the reality is, many people are just trying to get through the day. They don't feel empowered or successful. Rather, "survivors" keep their heads down and simply plod forward to survive.

However, many others are striving, sometimes because they enjoy what they do, and other times because they have received or are seeking gratification or a reward for hard work. "Strivers" gain headway because they are driven by progress, and when they see the fruit of their efforts, they see transformation in their lives.

PREPARE YOUR TEAM FOR POTENTIAL PROBLEMS, ESPECIALLY YOUR STRIVERS.

But striving isn't enough, because though strivers have more grit and capacity than survivors, they are thrown off and consumed with frustration when unforeseen problems make an appearance. Risk and change scare them.

"Thrivers" are fundamentally different in that they have learned to take risks, embrace the unknown, and embrace challenges as opportunities to grow.

So how can you create an environment that is conducive to producing a team of thrivers?

Prepare your team for potential problems, especially your strivers. Focus your training on what could go wrong and the steps that would need to be taken in the case of a sharp left turn. Revisit past problems and chronicle the action steps that were taken then that led you to victory.

When you openly give your organization permission to fail when they embrace change, your team will do much more than survive and strive.

They will thrive!

DAY 29

WHAT YOU'VE REAPED, YOU'VE SOWN

What grows in our lives is the physical manifestation of what we've planted.

We've heard that many times before. The Bible is wrought with the principles of sowing and reaping.

When we plant good seed, we grow good fruit. When we plant bad seed, we grow bad fruit.

Sometimes, we think we are planting good seed, only to learn later that the fruit is bitter.

It's a hard pill to swallow, but often, adversity is bred from unwise decisions.

I visited my friend Mike Poulin a while back.

During this visit, he shared a piece of wisdom with me that I have never forgotten. He said: "When we live our lives righteously and we make decisions that honor universal values, we receive the benefits of right thinking and of making good decisions; but when we make poor decisions and we don't treat others with value, then we receive the consequences of wrong thinking and poor decisions."

Let that sink in. We receive either the benefits or consequences of how we think and how we live our lives.

> **THE SOONER WE OWN OUR DECISIONS, THE SOONER WE ARE FREE TO CHANGE AND REAP BENEFITS RATHER THAN CONSEQUENCES.**

I thought about how true this is, and how easy it is to blame others, fate, or even God when things in life don't work out.

But most often the misfortunes we suffer are the result of our poor decisions.

I can almost instantly recall several business transactions and several very dear relationships that have failed in my life. At the time I blamed others, I blamed fate, and I'm ashamed to say that I blamed God, but in reality, the failures I experienced were simply consequences of my poor decisions.

Why is it so easy to blame God instead of ourselves? Do we really expect God to miraculously fix our self-inflicted problems?

Mike was right. Life has both benefits and consequences, and most of what we experience is a result of our thoughts, decisions, and actions. The sooner we own our decisions, the sooner we are free to change and reap benefits rather than consequences.

Yes, sometimes we can do everything right and still face tremendous challenges, as we live in a broken world. But more often than not, right thinking and right living produces benefits and protects us from negative consequences.

DAY 30

ONE IDEA DESERVES HOURS OF THOUGHT

Much of our life obligations require a lot of *doing*. We feed and care for our children each day; we go to work; we nurture our marriages.

Rarely do we consider that the quality of our doing is sculpted by a purposeful commitment to the quality of our *thinking*.

One day, a friend of mine encouraged me to devote four hours a day to thinking.

That seems like a lot, doesn't it?

You may be thinking what I was thinking.... *how could I possibly carve out four hours of time devoted to just thinking?*

It's possible that just isn't possible for you. At the very least, this principle depicts the importance of intentional, measured thought and reflection.

He expressed how my thinking ability was one of my greatest gifts, but that because I am also opportunity-driven and always finding and creating new solutions, there would always be tension emerging from endless opportunities that would compete with my thinking.... and if I wasn't careful and disciplined, my thinking gift would never be maximized.

ONE IDEA IS WORTHY OF FOUR HOURS OF THINKING.

As I have studied this, I have realized that for a highly creative person who feverishly takes action on their ideas, it takes immense discipline to mentally slow things down and process clearly. Even physiologically, when you solve a puzzle, endorphins are released in your brain—like a drug—and you naturally crave more of the "high" it produces.

It takes tremendous discipline to say no to new ideas, to slow down and think methodically, and to be willing to put nine out of ten good ideas on the shelf, and instead relentlessly make the tenth idea better. This will make all the difference for your business. One idea is worthy of four hours of thinking.

It's very likely that your business can only handle a couple of new ideas every few months, and it will serve you and your people better to share one or two good ideas that you have thought through rather than four or five. . . . and they likely would be unable to keep up with more than one or two.

My friend was the exemplar of disciplined thinking time. During his four hours, not even his assistant was allowed to interrupt him, and the reason?

He was convinced that any less than four hours of thinking would constitute as stealing from his organization. So, answer this honestly: Are you stealing from your organization?

DAY 31

PROVIDE SOLUTIONS, NOT JUST SERVICES

A re you a service or a solution?
As entrepreneurs, we start our business with the goal of providing a solution to a problem.

It could be a solution to an external problem or a solution to an internal problem.

We might find an innovative, time-saving way to accomplish a task, we might improve the quality of a service or product, or we might discover something new that we missed before (e.g., solve a problem we didn't know people had or solve a problem people didn't know they had).

We then develop this solution into a product and/or service that we can monetize, develop, and scale.

Here is where the trap is. . . . we begin to commoditize it, and when we commoditize it, our product or service loses its effectiveness.

WHEN ALL IS SAID AND DONE, WE CEASE TO BE A SOLUTION AND WE BECOME PEDDLERS OF SERVICE.

When we commoditize it, we become enticed to make a cooler, sexier, and more marketable product.

We focus on the product or service rather than the solution.

We fail to test every new widget or new service or functionality on the basis of how it solves the customer's problems more effectively and how it becomes a better solution.

When all is said and done, we cease to be a solution and we become peddlers of service.

We focus on impressing our customers rather than positively impacting their business. We stop listening and instead focus more on output rather than outcomes.

We have to keep our eye on the ball, friends. Our most valuable commodity is people.

Every business decision, every team meeting, every new idea, and every systematic restructure should be approached with people in mind.

If we aren't asking the question, "How will this add value to peoples' lives?" then we are missing the purpose of business—not to mention, the most rewarding part of it.

Be a solution and fight to stay a solution.

It takes tremendous discipline, but the reward will be in the trust you establish and the impact you will have.

Because people are more interested in your solution than your service.

TAKEAWAY

Think about when you have transitioned from surviving to striving and then striving to thriving. What did you do that was different? How does it make you feel to take responsibility for the outcomes in your life? Do you designate time for thinking without distraction? In what ways do you think this practice may produce positive change in your life? In what ways have you prioritized providing services over solutions? How could you begin to provide solutions instead of services?

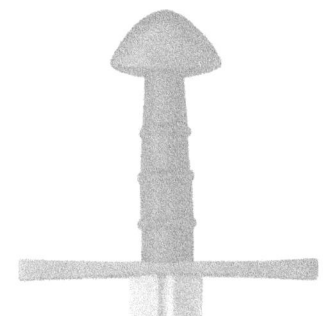

PART 8
INSPIRATION

DAY 32

HOPE HAS A FAMILY

St. Augustine has been quoted saying, "Hope has two daughters: courage and discontent."

This is a pretty thought-provoking statement. Without courage, there is no hope, and there is no hope in the cozy bed of contentment.

What feels good isn't always good. In fact, the things that feel the best are sometimes the most harmful.

Contentment is a complex concept. Paul inspires us to learn to be content in all things and in all circumstances. Here, contentment brings peace, joy, and a sense of purpose that is unattached to how big or how important your assignment is throughout the passing seasons of life.

Contentment only becomes a problem when it is rooted in complacency. Complacency is comfortable. Complacency is easy. It requires no effort, no risk, and no discomfort.

And here's the kicker: Discomfort waters the seeds of hope.

HOPE REQUIRES THE COURAGE TO CHALLENGE THE STATUS QUO.

Hope looks forward to a better future, but this requires change, and there are few things we humans resist more than change. Change takes courage, believing in a cause, confronting the status quo, and pursuing the unknown.

As human beings, we desire security, and we fear risk. Our hearts want safety—a predictable future—and our minds want to understand, "What will happen tomorrow?"

Hope requires the courage to challenge the status quo. Hope requires us to oppose the certainties of life. Hope requires us to accept our present condition as unacceptable. True hope can see the good in the present but is yet fortified with confidence that there is more to achieve, to experience, and to be. Hope is innately produced by a "happy discontent", rooted in belief in our own potential.

When we believe there is more to life than where we currently sit, we will birth both courage and discontent together, a perfect union to produce a hope that will sustain and propel us toward a life of significance.

DAY 33

THERE'S NO PLACE LIKE THE PRESENT

If you've come this far, I hope you are starting to see how important and valuable misfortune and hardship are in shaping and molding our future into a masterpiece.

I want to demonstrate a case in point.

A few weeks ago, I toured an amazing ministry. Our tour guide was passionate, raw, and humble, yet confident.

He shared a bit of his story. Over the last thirty-six years, he had been in prison five times, stabbed many times, and shot, landing him in a coma for three months.

Despite these hardships and setbacks, his heart was filled with joy because it took him on a five-year journey of re-inventing his life. He began teaching courses on anger management and mentoring others who wrestle with the same set of challenges that he did.

> **SOMETIMES WE BEAT A DEAD HORSE WHEN WE COULD RIDE AWAY ON ONE INSTEAD.**

His three-year plan was to become a firefighter. But most of all, he was proud to be reunited with his children and eager to become a loving father.

As he shared his story, his spirit glowed with a deep, joyful energy. He talked about the power of living in the moment. He said that he used to be so worried about the past that he tripped over himself in the present. He said that if God wanted us to look backward, he would have put eyes on the back of our heads.

There's a very specific reason why we look backward when we are walking through an oppressive present.

No matter where you've come from, backward is a familiar place. You've already been there, and where you've already been helps you make sense of where you are and where you are going.

There's some truth to this. But sometimes we beat a dead horse when we could ride away on one instead.

This man's breakthrough came when he stopped focusing on surviving and instead started slowing down to live in the present.

There is power in the present and when we are at peace with where we are, we position ourselves to walk into a better and brighter future.

DAY 34

SIGNIFICANCE STARTS WITH YOU

We can't put success and significance in the same basket. While they cannot be detangled, they are fundamentally two different principles for living a healthy life.

Here's where they differ: Success is all about self.... significance is about others.

THE CONSEQUENCE IS THAT WHEN WE DON'T VALUE OURSELVES, WE ARE INCAPABLE OF VALUING OTHERS.

A friend of mine once said that significant people are successful people who have grown up and matured. It all starts with our values.

If we value ourselves, we will value others.

This may seem backward. Isn't success about others? It is, but people who "chase false value"—material possessions, power, or prestige—don't really value themselves. They cling to a "scoreboard" to satisfy the lack of value they feel for themselves.

The consequence is that when we don't value ourselves, we are incapable of valuing others.

That's not real success.

It has been said that you must be successful first before you can be significant, because you can't give to others what you don't first have. That's only partially true because success is an inside work before it is anything else. It starts with you.

I have often talked about the journey of life, specifically from a career or "life stage" perspective.

We start out in our mid-20s just trying to **Survive**.

With some hard work and moderate discipline, we can achieve some **Stability**.

If we work hard enough, if we have some grit or determination, we can achieve a level of **Success**.

We can then choose to focus more on giving than attaining and devote a big part of our lives and wealth to serving others—this puts us on the path to **Significance**.

While these four steps give us a path or a template, most people won't go past the Success stage.

Those who make these shifts had this value of self, expressed through service to others, instilled in them earlier in their life—maybe in their childhood—or, perhaps they were fortunate enough to have them modeled later in life.

Spend time around those who model those values and start shifting.

Significance starts with you.

TAKEAWAY

Where does hope stand in your life? Do you find yourself full of it? In lack of it? In what ways are you challenging yourself to exit your comfort zone? How could you rise to that challenge moving forward? What kind of narratives have you written in your past that you have taken into your present? What do you think your life could look like if you were to be freed from your past? In what ways are you pursuing success over significance and why?

PART 9
LEADERSHIP LESSONS

DAY 35

THERE IS ROOM ON THE MOUNTAIN FOR CLIMBERS AND GUIDES

f you have picked up this book, you likely fall into one of two categories (or perhaps, you identify with one more than the other): You are presently in a leadership position or, while you may not desire a "top dog" kind of position, you are interested in being part of a leadership team.

Both are leaders. Leaders come in all shapes and sizes.

Regardless of where you fall on this leadership continuum, something is driving you to lead. Some leaders are more focused on the ultimate goal. Others are more driven by the people they get to push toward the goal. Both are valuable and want to see their team win.

But some find being up front and center of the team more appealing. I like to call these leaders "core performers". They love challenges. They love to win. They love to see how far and fast they can go. They are climbers.

Others are guides. They love to bring people with them on the journey.

CLIMBERS, ARE YOU UTILIZING YOUR GUIDES? GUIDES, ARE YOU FOLLOWING YOUR CLIMBERS?

Guides travel at a slower pace than climbers. They have a different goal because they don't see the same terrain that climbers see (even if they are on the same mountain). Guides are not just interested in how far they can go. They are more interested in how far they can go with the people they have chosen to bring with them.

Whatever the reason, guides lead less from a competitive nature and more from a relational nature. They desire companionship more than achievement. They are married to their purpose: developing and growing people. That fuels them and fulfills them much more deeply than arriving at a destination

(but believe me—we need the climbers. It's challenging to develop others without someone who knows the end goal!)

If you're a guide, know this: traveling at a slower pace with the right people by your side pays off. There will likely come a day when you can no longer travel on your own and those whom you brought with you can finish what you started, traveling longer and further.

If you are a guide, make sure you bring not just anyone alongside you, but the right people.

If you are a climber, make sure your guides know the direction of your destination.

Climbers, are you utilizing your guides? Guides, are you following your climbers?

DAY 36

LEADERSHIP IS DISAPPOINTING PEOPLE

There is a truth about leadership that can be a hard pill to swallow:

Leadership isn't about not disappointing people. Disappointment is inevitable.

It's about disappointing them in a way that still communicates their value, and in a way that they can handle.

For a relational leader like me, this is a very hard concept to grasp and accept. I love so many of my people, especially those who have been by my side for the long haul, and I believe in them.

I'm sure many of you can relate.

But a very important part of my job is to define what each person on my team does best and understand the limits of their capacity.

This may sound contrary to most self-help literature, that we should "believe in people and give them opportunities to grow", but that also means protecting them and the company from the pain of avoidable failure. All growth has a cost, and sometimes we make the mistake of giving someone a task or assignment that they simply can't perform, and their failure then becomes our fault.

Sometimes, disappointment can cause offense and a feeling of failure in those you choose to withhold assignments from that exceed their abilities. However, this response could not be more far removed from the true intention.

IT'S OFTEN BETTER TO DISAPPOINT SOMEONE IN THE SHORT-TERM THAN RISK LOSING THEM LONG TERM.

And the true intention is this: We owe it to the business and that person to give them what they can handle (but *not* at the expense of the growth that comes with a good challenge)—not set them up for failure.

When we give people an opportunity that is "above their capacity" and they start to drown, they often revert to blaming others rather than looking in the mirror. The pain of the failure and of letting you down can blind their self-awareness.

Self-awareness is key to growth. The more self-aware your people are, the easier it will be to coach them. At times, your decisions will disappoint them, especially if they aren't self-aware.

Manage your people carefully and remember, it's often better to disappoint someone in the short-term than risk losing them long term.

DAY 37

EVEN GOOD SOLDIERS SOMETIMES DIE

In many ways, business can mimic war.

And sometimes, good soldiers die in the battle.

But good soldiers do not have to lose their dignity in the process. And as their leader, you have the privilege and responsibility of keeping their dignity intact.

How many times have you heard of a company that hit a wall and had to downsize, lay off staff, close a division, or completely shut their doors?

Maybe this has been your story and hits close to home.

Most of those affected were good, hard workers. They were good soldiers, but their company lost a battle, or maybe even lost the war.

THE ARMY HONORS THE FALLEN SOLDIERS AFTER THE BATTLE.

Great leaders truly care about their people. They develop and task their HR teams to train and develop them. They intentionally and regularly "walk slowly through the crowd" in the office to connect and encourage them. They feel a deep responsibility to provide a promising future for them and their families.

That's why it hurts so much when they have to let go or lay off good people.

I was reminded of the story of an army general in WWII who, after sending a company of soldiers into battle—a battle he knew was necessary to the war effort that they would likely lose—would physically throw up outside before returning to his commanding tent after sending out his troops.

Though I have never sent soldiers out into battle, I have been forced to lay off people whom I care deeply for, even a week before Christmas in order to pay the rest of the company within ninety days.

Here's the lesson:

The army honors the fallen soldiers after the battle. While it's usually unpreventable when good soldiers die, it's devastating when no one attends their funeral.

So, the next time you need to lay off a good worker or close an office, honor the workers publicly and personally reach out to their family afterwards. If you can, assure their spouse and kids that the worker was not at fault and do your best to help them find a new opportunity somewhere else.

Do that well, and they will feel they have been given a second chance at life.

DAY 38

THE MORAL AUTHORITY OF LEADERSHIP

Most leaders are doers by some measure.

"Doing" is what creates their initial success. They see an opportunity and they seize it, and this produces success most of the time. But as their organizations grow, they need to commit to raising up leaders or they will hit a ceiling.

That's because doers always work for thinkers. Doers attract other doers, and talent attracts talent, and as long as you are competing with your leaders for results, you will ultimately place a lid on them or risk losing credibility with them.

IF YOU DON'T THINK AHEAD OF YOUR PEOPLE, IF YOU DON'T SEE THINGS THAT THEY DON'T YET SEE, YOU LOSE THE MORAL AUTHORITY TO LEAD THEM.

The day you stop thinking better than or ahead of your team is the day you lose the moral authority to lead them, because they are looking to you for answers.

This is where the morality piece comes in: Thinking ahead of those you lead will teach them, by example, how to think ahead of those they will lead in the future.

Let me repeat that again—if you don't think ahead of your people, if you don't see things that they don't yet see, you lose the moral authority to lead them.

And thinking takes time and work (at times quite taxing work), but it must be done if you wish to lead from a place of leadership impartation.

In a sense, those who have earned moral authority leave a legacy of leadership characterized by moral authority.

When you make meaningful and game-changing discoveries about and for your business, your people will respect you and follow you because you took the time to think them through.

Think ahead and secure your moral authority to lead your team.

Think ahead and give your team the opportunity to become leaders in your industry.

TAKEAWAY

Who are your mountain climbers? Who are your guides? In what ways do you see them working together, and how do their strengths and weaknesses impact the team as a whole? Does your team understand that the assignments they receive are important, no matter how small? When have you had to make a tough call in the past that greatly impacted someone? How did you handle the aftermath? How have you or how have you not demonstrated your moral authority to your team?

PART 10
TEAMWORK

DAY 39

BUILD THE PLAN WITH YOUR CUSTOMER

When you are selling, you are not selling a service or a product, but a partnership.

I do a lot of presentations, where I speak to various dealership groups or at business centers.

It goes without saying, but the first thing I do is call them. I present them with a plan to help them sell more cars. But my strategy has vastly changed over time. The new strategy is more effective, more collaborative, and more rewarding.

I used to over-prepare—I had the perfect plan in place, all mapped out in PDFs, charts, and graphs in advance. And that's all I had. But I've learned over time that there's a MUCH better way:

Build the plan *with* the customer rather than bring the plan *to* them. It's far more powerful.

> **TELLING POTENTIAL CUSTOMERS WHAT THEY NEED CAN ACTUALLY ERODE THEIR TRUST IN THE VALUE OF YOUR SERVICE.**

Preparation is still important when you enter a meeting. Believe me, I make sure I have all of my assets in proper order and ready to go!

But now, I also bring a good old-fashioned clean sheet of paper (or even a napkin!) and a pen, and I engage them. I ask questions about their problems. I suggest different solutions. And then, we build the plan *together*.

Telling potential customers what they need can actually erode their trust in the value of your service.

Lending potential customers the freedom and space to tell *you* what they need will open their hearts to hearing how you believe your service could meet that need.

I still prepare before a meeting, but many times, I don't use half of what I've prepared. But what do I do? I go there to listen and build the plan with them. I make sure my soul is calm so that I can focus on listening more to what they are buying rather than pitch what I am selling.

When you build a plan together, customer buy-in will go through the roof because it's no longer *your* plan, but *their* plan.

Think about a potential client or customer you are hoping to do business with now.

Could you recite their needs if you were asked to? Would they leave feeling like you get it, or would they feel like something was left out?

Listen more and talk less.

DAY 40

F.A.T.T.

At the beginning of this book, we discussed how the incubation and realization of good ideas start with writing ideas down.

There's a step in between writing your ideas down and creating solutions.

You must take new ideas and filter them through the "F.A.T.T" principle of actualizing ideas:

1) Feelings. Attend to how the idea makes you feel. Great ideas should excite you—and that's a good sign. But elation can be dangerous when it becomes impulsivity. Emotions can be deceptive. So, take at least twenty-four hours before you take action on a new idea.

2) Agreement. Twenty-four hours later, reach out to two people whom you believe could evaluate the idea wisely to get agreement. Then, have *them* mull over it for a day

or two. Don't demand an immediate answer. They will either come back to you with agreement or pushback.
3) Thinking. At this stage, you have received either agreement or pushback. Regardless of the response, take another twenty-four hours and consider how you can take the idea and make it better.
4) Timing. Ask yourself: Is it the right time to implement the idea? If you feel confident that the timing is right, arrange a company brainstorm session, because the wrong timing can screw up a great idea.

JUST REMEMBER THIS: SEEKING WISE COUNSEL WILL BUFFER AGAINST THE TEMPTATION TO RUSH INTO A VENTURE THAT MAY ULTIMATELY DAMAGE YOU, YOUR ORGANIZATION, AND YOUR PEOPLE.

Write down your ideas and keep a "F.A.T.T" diary. Put these principles into practice.

But don't stop there!

Share your "F.A.T.T" experiences with others—both the good and the bad—so that you and your team can work together to make adjustments.

F.A.T.T is meant to serve as a guideline or template for how to leverage a new idea to enhance your business. Good blueprints also afford a great deal of flexibility to color outside the lines.

Just remember this: seeking wise counsel will buffer against the temptation to rush into a venture that may ultimately damage you, your organization, and your people. It may also provide the environment for you to mature a good idea until the time is right.

TAKEAWAY

Think about the times when you have had the most success with a client or customer. Think about the worst experiences you've had with a client or customer. What would you attribute to the different outcomes? What could you have done differently to promote trust and credibility? How do you turn your ideas into realities? What is your process? Is it effective? What modifications need to be made for greater success?

F.A.T.T.

www.ingramcontent.com/pod-product-compliance
Lightning Source LLC
Chambersburg PA
CBHW070535090426
42735CB00013B/2992